# 30 VALUABLE LESSONS OF LIFE: TRUE AND WORKING ADVICE THAT WILL CHANGE YOUR LIFE

Alan C & Ann G

# DEDICATION

This Book is dedicated to the strongest person I have known
My Grandmother.

# CONTENTS

Be unique, believe In everyday kindness ….

# 1. DECLUTTER YOUR MIND.

We are living in a world full of technologies that serve us information constantly. How many of you have learned how to avoid information you do not require or how to take one/two hours of your day to disconnect yourself from the bombardment of information into your subconscious mind. Learn to choose what is required and filter out the negative or unnecessary information this would give your mind a positive assertiveness.

# 2. DECLUTTER YOUR HOME.

We are so used to accumulating material things, it has become very difficult to get rid of things that we no longer require or use. Have you noticed all these items are only consuming space around you and not adding any value to your life? Go ahead try cleaning this mess and get rid of things that add no value or is of no future use to you. This will bring a positive impact on your mind and surrounding.

# 3. MAKE YOUR BED EVERY MORNING

Organized bedroom gives you better sleep and a positive mindset. This will help you wake up refreshed, this is a simple yet surprising habit to develop. Once you set this habit in momentum the benefits are many. When you make your bed everyday morning it helps you get the feeling that you have achieved one task and this will give you the mindset to achieve more. Let's say you had a bad day when you are back home at least you have a made bed.

# 4. FIX WHAT NEEDS AND CAN BE FIXED

Don't we all have a broken lamp or a kitchen appliance that just sits around and waits to be fixed? We are all aware of their condition but we keep telling our self " I will do it tomorrow or after a few days ". Such tomorrow's rarely come. What we need here is an attitude change. Learn to accept that if something needs action from your end and if this action can resolve it, then you have to take that action without leaving an excuse behind. Once you have understood this concept you can significant changes in your home and relations.

# 5. EXERCISE, A SIMPLE DECISION A LONG LASTING IMPACT ON LIFE.

You, me and a vast majority of people depend on a 9-6 job which is most of the time sedentary. This leads to various health issues and shockingly few among them are Cancer, Sugar, and your sex life slows down. Exercising daily can help each one of us reduce various health risks and utilize and keep our body in the best possible shape.

# 6. THE MAGIC OF MORNING ROUTINE

Waking up and just going with the flow is a dumb way of living in this fast-paced world. Time is of the essence and it is money. Every day try imagining how your day should go from the moment you wake up until the end of your day. This way you will lose less time deciding and doing the unnecessary task and can use your precious time to have a fulfilled day

# 7. HOW SLEEP CHANGES YOUR LIFE.

This is where an organized bedroom comes to help. You may have come home from a hard day at work but you have a ready bed which for sure makes you feel better. But the trick that you have to understand is avoiding any unnecessary negative conversations or thoughts before bedtime as many of you might not know that these thoughts remain in one's subconscious mind and can affect your mood and in a long run your life. So even though you might think it's a small change but it would have a large impact on your life. Remember good sleep can help you have a better start the next day.

# 8. LEARN SOMETHING NEW.

We learn while we live. It is always interesting to learn something new and to get a new skill added to our list of existing. Who can say someday this might be helpful. It is always advisable to learn something that can add value to your life. Such small skills together can add value to your personality. This would be helpful in some or the other at some or the other time and then you would think and smile how a small act made a big impact.

# 9. KEY TO BETTER HEALTH

By doing this you won't only be sure you are eating healthy food, but you will enjoy food more. Don't be shocked if I tell you that you can save more than 2,500$ per year only by preparing and taking your own lunch to work. I believe for an average person this is a significant saving. There is also another angle to this, that is you now decide what you consume and what your food contains let it be more protein diet, fewer carbs. Now the wheel to a healthy body is in your hands and up to you to lead it in the right direction.

# 10. HOW 30 MINS MAKES A DIFFERENCE.

Are you among the majority who puts the alarm in snooze button to enjoy another 15 – 30 mins of nice and peaceful sleep, Well then you are going to hate this. Every day make it a point to wake up 30 mins earlier than your current schedule. This extra 30 mins every day you get will become a game changer if you use it wisely. Feel free to spend this 30 mins how every you like but I would suggest using it for doing something productive or anything you love. It will for sure improve your mood and lifestyle. Think about it for a while and set your alarm 30 mins earlier.

# 11. TAKE A BREAK, IT MATTERS !!

It is totally fine to take a short break at work or at home if you feel that you are drained. Find a few minutes take a deep breath and relax this will help you regain the lost energy. Remember if you are drained or exhausted then your mind would not be performing at its peak and this can lead to wrong decisions at work or mood swings at home. So it's really necessary that you give your mind time to recharge and regain and help reach its normal performance level.

# 12. MOTIVATION, WE ALL NEED IT SOMETIME.

Sometimes we all need a little tap on our back or a gentle push towards our goals. In this world which is so chaotic, we all run out of motivation at some point and that is when you fall. You need to find what motivates you and remind yourself during these times. This will help you get up and brush off the dust and start from where you have left. Motivation can be a video, an e-book or a family.

# 13. RECONNECT WITH YOUR TRUE FRIENDS.

More than 1000 friends and followers in social media but only a handful whom you can depend on if you need a friend. You all have that one friend who was always there with you during your good time and bad times but as time passed somehow you lost touch. Since there is a gap that has come between you guys now it's hard to reconnect. But remember gaps are meant to be bridged and it's fine if you are the first one to put effort to reconnect.

# 14. LISTEN TO SOOTHING MUSIC.

It's proved that music improves your mood and relaxes you. Everyone loves music and have their own taste which differs from individual to individual. Why not give this a try "listen to music that is soothing, this will calm your mind and give you a relaxed feel". Our eardrums are always bombarded with honking, noise from outside and the new gen music but the real result of music can be felt when you listen to soothing ones. For example, listen to rainfall sound or flute.

# 15. YOUR OWN HAPPINESS PROJECT

Isn't life all about being happy. Then make a list of things that make you happy. Once you have it ready go through it, you will be surprised how even those things that you consider little makes you happy. Try to focus your energy and time on doing more of these things in life which will eventually make you a happy person. Only once you know your goal can you reach there similarly only if you know what makes you happy, you know what are the things to do and things to avoid.

# 16. LAUGH AT LIFE.

"A good laugh and a long sleep are two best cures", Watch a cartoon or read a joke or call your best friend and tell him/her about the time you both goofed up or had a good time. Try to laugh at least once a day or try to make other's laugh. A laugh is contagious and who knows it might make another person's day. Don't believe me imagine a small baby smiling at you that smile will replicate on your face.

# 17. BIG DATA HAS CHANGED THE GAME

Big data aka "information" that you are always around you in different forms such as social media feeds, daily news, work emails, or advertisements. They all have an impact on your thinking Try to surround yourself with books, music and positive information that describe what you want to be, how you have to get there, what actions are required from your end to reach there. The information you are surrounded should act as a tool to help you get there and not the other way around. (Not dragging you into a circle of negativity ). In short, we have information in our fingertips but it's for us to choose what we require.

Gather, analyze and use this information to reach your goals.

# 18. TREAT YOURSELF LIKE A KING.

When was the last time you treated yourself with a gift or something you love? A large majority of people spend time and money on making their loved one happy. Well, you to deserve to be treated the same way once in a while. Most of you agree life is unpredictable and short at certain times. Then why hold back from bringing a smile on your own face. By doing so you are not only making yourself happy but also encouraging the people around you to do the same. Let's hope this habit spread like wildfire and result in a happy society.

# 19. THERE IS  LIFE AROUND YOU, DISCOVER IT.

Every day you wake up and get to do the repetitive tasks which you always have been doing. Like waking up every day and going to work, coming back home exhausted and going to bed. Well, many of you can relate to this lifestyle.  It's isn't your fault that you have got caught in the cobweb of life and work.

Take some time off and go for a walk in a park, go for a picnic with your friends and family. Remember there is life out there waiting for you than this repetitive lifestyle you lead. You will be able to enjoy it only if you find time to break the monotonous schedule.

# 20. FIND A HIDDEN GEM

Pick a book or two in a month and read them every day.
It will rekindle your curiosity and make your brain function better. When I say pick a book I don't mean magazines or entertainment magazines which are filled with information that does not add any value. Ask yourself what value or good does it bring to you if you come to know what the celebrity loves to wear or eat. These are all pure marketing to make you follow the consumeristic lifestyle. Instead, read a book that would make you think and help to develop yourself.

# 21. MYSTERIOUS POWER OF GOOD DEED

Besides the fact that you are helping someone you are also bringing a warm feeling over your heart which makes you feel good. It will give you a new perspective about the world around you. You understand that you are not the only person who is faced with problems. This small act will remind you that many out there are going through much worse problems than your own. Every action you give out will come back to you so isn't it better to give out a good deed to expect good back in return.

# 22. "ONE WORD" BIG IMPACT - GRATITUDE

Why express gratitude? because it's the right thing to do. You should learn to express gratitude in your professional as well as your personal life. This small expression can enhance our own life but also make the other person feel appreciated. Do remember that when you express gratitude it should be from your heart. Gratitude is give-and-take act that serves as a basis for any relation business/personal.

eg: "Thank you" for taking the time to read this book.

# 23. LEAVE WORK AT WORK.

So much stress we face nowadays has to do with the inability of the brain to let go of things. We, humans, are still figuring out how to develop this habit. Work stress is a byproduct of all the fears and thoughts we give life to by hanging on them and contemplating about them relentlessly. The moment you leave work or your working hour is over learn to stop thinking about it. Breath and relax before you reach home. Work-life balance is essential for a happy life. So decide from today and find out ways to leave work at work. This will improve the quality of life significantly.

# 24. NECESSITY OF QUALITY "ME TIME"

You and I know that self-care is essential for happiness. For each one of us, this would be different, well if you ask me I would say whatever ritual that relaxes you is "me-time". And why is it we need time for ourselves. it is proven that a small bit of alone time reboots your brain, improves concentration, makes us more productive, gives space for self-discovery. One of the major reason for unhappy married life is lack of privacy or "me-time". Find time in your busy schedule and block your calendar for some quality me time. It's the quality of "me-time" and not the quantity that matters.

# 25. TODO LIST.

If you know what all are pending to be done this will help you plan and execute them in a structured way. Remember that lists are a great way to organize your information and give them the priority. Once you have them arranged and structured in a proper manner, now you know which one has to be tackled first. If all the items in your list cannot be dealt in a day its fine, break them in parts so you can finish what is urgent the early and leave the not so important ones for the next day. What happens if you don't have this. You forget and the thing you forgot could be important and listing and tackling removes this issue.

# 26. TAKE PHOTOS

Don't we all have those really old photos which we come across by mistake and when we see it we remember that good time we had with our parents, family or friends.
In a world of countless selfies and snap's. I tell you to capture the moment that really matters. Take a photo of your family, capture these good times so you can take a look after some years and smile.

# 27. CREATE A SPENDING PLAN

We all buy things that actually don't need and spend a lot of our hard earned income on these items. One reason for this is impulse spending. You need to make a budget plan and try to stick to it. This will help you identify if you have enough money to do things that you need to do or would like to do. It gives you a clear picture of what you have and what can be done with it and what can be avoided. By doing so we avoid sinking deeper and deeper into debt trap every year.

# 28. BREATH

Do you know this is what keeps you alive? And this could save your sanity. It is said that when negative emotions are high the breathing becomes short and shallow. Learn breathing technique and try deep breathing exercises, this can change your life drastically. Doing regular breathing techniques has many benefits such as it will relax your muscles, oxygen to your body increases, detoxification improves and blood pressure lowers.

# 29. VIST NEW PLACES EVERY YEAR

At least once a year plan to visit a place you haven't seen before. You live only once and the worlds a big place why not cover as much as possible.

# 30. POWER OF COMPOUNDING

Don't underestimate the power of having a peaceful mind that you have saved some money to weather any storm. By saving early would give you an idea that you and your family have a cushion set already, in case if there is a fall (let's hope not). Many of us are worried because of tight financial situation and trust me it's a danger in disguise as it continues, it can lead a number of issues such as it will have a negative impact on your peace of mind leading to stress, more stress leads to more financial problems and this can lead to issues to erupt in family as the emotions are high. Save and invest money at an early age.

<u>THANK YOU.</u>